Heather Hammond's
funky flute

A course for young beginners

Book 1

Illustrated by Melody-Anne Lee

Funky Flute Books 1 and 2 will take you from your very first lesson in Book 1 to around grade 2 level in Book 2. There are many interesting pieces, including some for ensemble playing. There are also exercises to improve technique, listening games and puzzles.

The Teacher's Book has piano accompaniments and the CD provides backing tracks to help you sound great when you practise at home.

Funky Flute Repertoire provides an additional range of new and well-known pieces.

Have fun!

Special thanks to Janet Butler for technical expertise and to Emily Hunnybun and Catherine Thompson for trying things out.

First published in Great Britain in 2007 by Kevin Mayhew Ltd
Buxhall, Stowmarket, Suffolk IP14 3BW
Tel: +44 (0) 1449 737978 Fax: +44 (0) 1449 737834
E-mail: info@kevinmayhewltd.com

© Copyright 2007 Kevin Mayhew Ltd.
ISBN 978 184867 098 3
ISMN M 57024 727 1 Catalogue No. 3612133
6 7 8 9

Illustration and design: Melody-Anne Lee
Music Setter: Donald Thomson
Editor and proof reader: Sarah Stirling

Printed and bound in Great Britain

Key to symbols

CD track.

Complete has flute part.

Backing has no flute part.

Exercises that will help you play rhythmically.

Exercises that will help you listen carefully.

Exercises that will help you to get a good sound and help your breath control.

Exercise patterns for getting to know the notes.

Contents

3

You've chosen to play the flute!
Great choice!

The flute is the oldest of all the woodwind instruments.
The history probably dates back to the ninth century BC.

You can play different types of music on the flute and it's very easy to carry around . . .

In this book you'll learn how to hold the flute, get a really good sound, find out how to read music and learn lots of fun pieces.

First of all . . .

Your flute will be in three pieces. These are:

the **Head Joint** (the part that you blow into).

the **Middle Joint** (the longest part) and the **Foot Joint.**

Your first sound . . .

Try to get your first sound by using the head joint only.
Hold the head joint with the open end to the right.
This is what your mouth should look like when looking in a mirror:

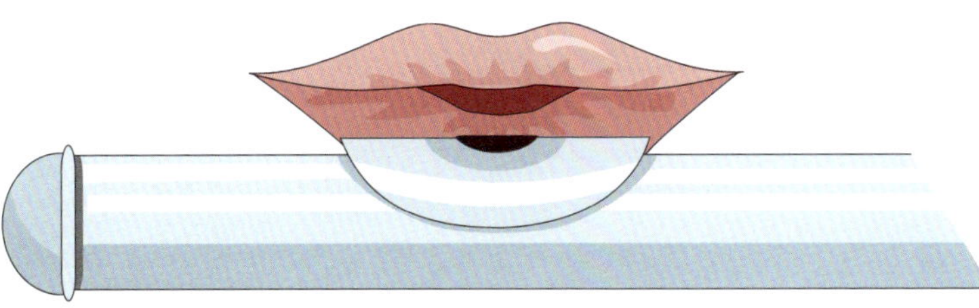

Create a small gap between your lips and blow gently across the top of the
blow hole whilst gently pressing your bottom lip onto the lip plate.
Say 't' (as in tongue) as you start to blow.
This is called '**tonguing**'.

Keep your mouth as relaxed as you can and the gap between your lips as small as possible.
Try to improve the sound you are making by twisting the head joint closer or further away from you.

When you are making a good sound try playing different types of notes

Long notes

Take a deep breath and blow gently trying to keep the gap between your lips as small as you can so that none of the air is wasted.

Keep the air flow steady and always listen to try and get the best sound. The practising of long notes is really good for flute players. You'll find lots of Long Note Practice Sessions later in this book.

Soft notes

Begin by taking a big breath but let the air out very slowly and evenly to get a gentle and soft sound.
Keep listening to get the nicest sound you can!

Short notes

First take a big breath and then put the tip of your tongue onto the back of your front, top teeth.

Get ready to breathe out and then move your tongue away from your teeth by saying 't'; but then stop the air flow quickly to stop the sound and make the notes short.
Take a breath when you need to but not between every note.

Loud notes

Take a big breath again but this time force the air out quickly.
You might not be able to play a very long note because your air supply will run out much quicker! Make sure that the gap remains small between your lips.

When you are getting a good sound most of the time it's time to begin . . .

Putting your flute together

This must be done carefully – you don't want to damage your instrument!
Place the **Head Joint** into the **Middle Joint** and gently line up the centre of the blow hole with the first key on the middle joint:

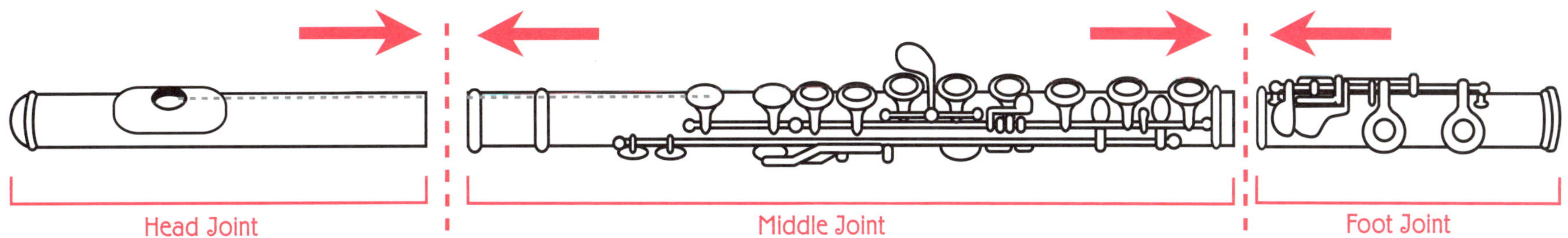

Then place the **Foot Joint** onto the **Middle Joint** lining up as shown here

This is a treble clef – you will always find one at the beginning of a line of flute music.

Music notes are written on lines and in spaces.
There are always 5 lines and this is called a stave.

Music is written in bars. They are separated by bar lines.
You will find a double bar line at the end of the music.

This is a one beat note – a crotchet. You play a sound that lasts for one beat.

$\frac{4}{4}$ You will find 2 numbers after the treble clef. It's called the time signature.
This one tells you that there will be four crotchet beats in each bar.

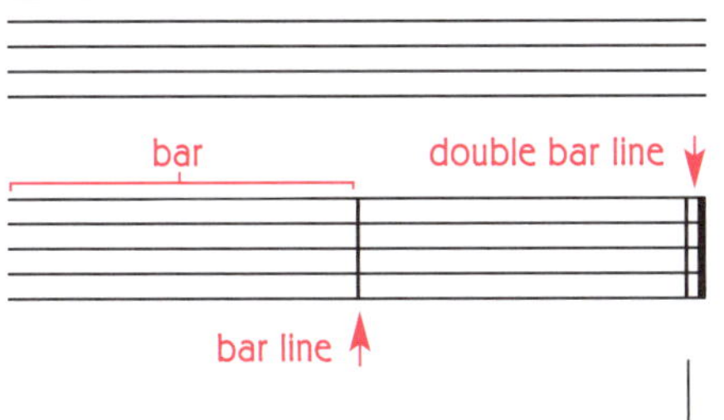

It's important to be able to feel a regular, steady beat.
Practise clapping a steady crotchet-beat rhythm along with the track.

How to hold your flute

Your left hand MUST go at the top (even if you are left-handed).
Place your fingers gently over the correct keys as shown (right)
Don't actually press any of the keys down yet.

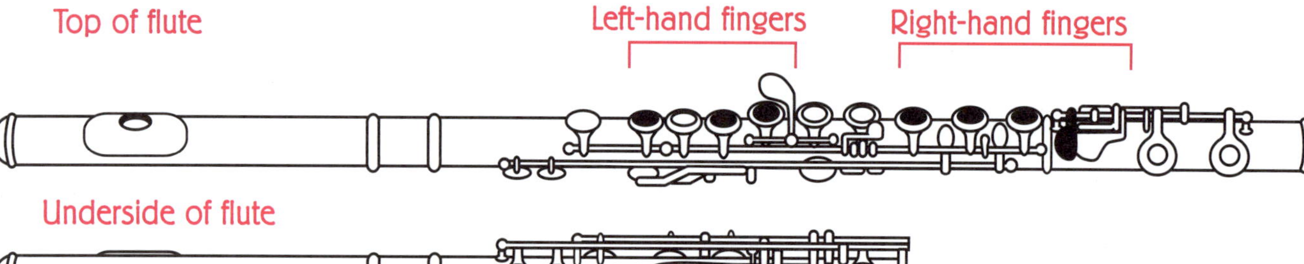

How to hold your flute

Your right-hand thumb and your left-hand forefinger should take the weight of your flute.

Your right-hand thumb presses against the underneath of your flute beneath your right-hand forefinger.

The tip of the forefinger of your left hand is positioned over the key but the rest of that finger curves around so that your first finger joint presses firmly against the body of the flute helping to support it.

(Don't let your right-hand forefinger curve around in this way – the first finger joint shouldn't touch the rods on the side of your flute).

Don't take any of the weight with your left-hand thumb – eventually you will learn notes that require your thumb to move to the key further up the flute or even ones requiring the thumb to be completely off the keys.

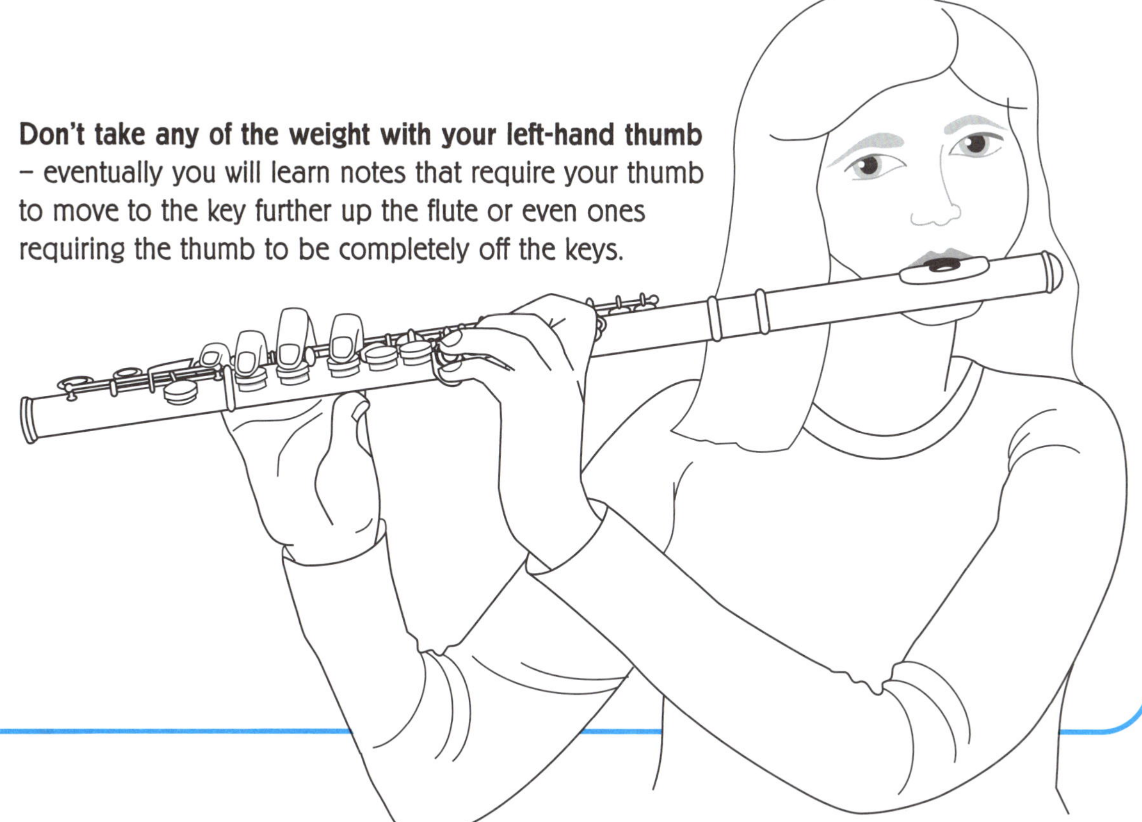

Posture

Tilt your head and the flute a little to the right and turn your head very slightly towards your left shoulder.

Make sure that your right elbow is well away from your body so that your flute is nearly horizontal.

When you're tired you may find that your elbow gradually drops to your waist – try to make sure this doesn't happen!

It's a good idea to look in a mirror and check your posture from time to time.

SET 1
First note – B

This is what B looks like on the stave

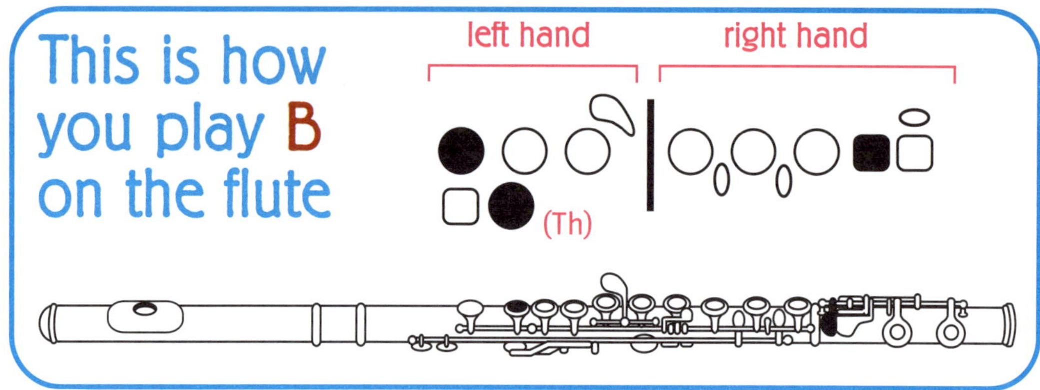

Now you can practise keeping a steady beat again along with the CD track, but this time play the note B on your flute.

Steady Eddie

 Just B soft and slow   

Soft and slow

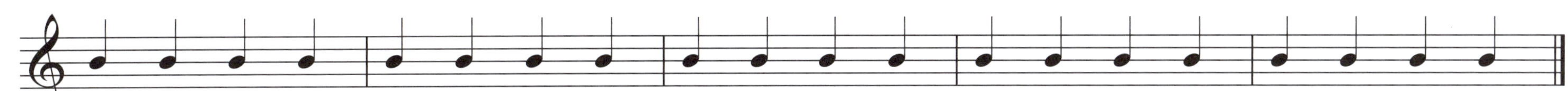

Just B loud and fast    

Loud and fast

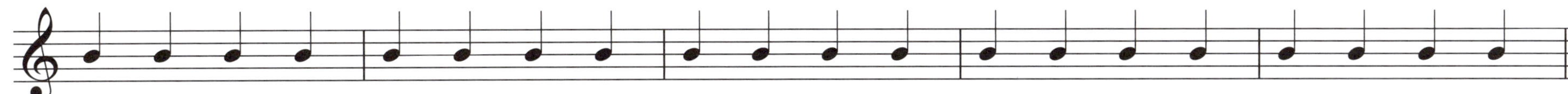

11

This is a **crotchet rest**.
You have to be silent for one beat.

Practise clapping each of the following rhythms 4 times. Then clap the whole thing through twice with the CD accompaniment.

This sign tells you to be silent for a certain number of bars in the music. This one means don't play for four whole bars. Often another instrument will be playing whilst you are being silent.

In the next piece don't play anything for the first 4 bars – listen to the piano introduction and then start playing at bar 5 – you'll need to count really carefully!

Bluesy B

12

What will be?

This is a two-beat note – a **minim**.

This is a **minim rest** – you have to be silent for 2 beats (It sits on the middle line of the stave)

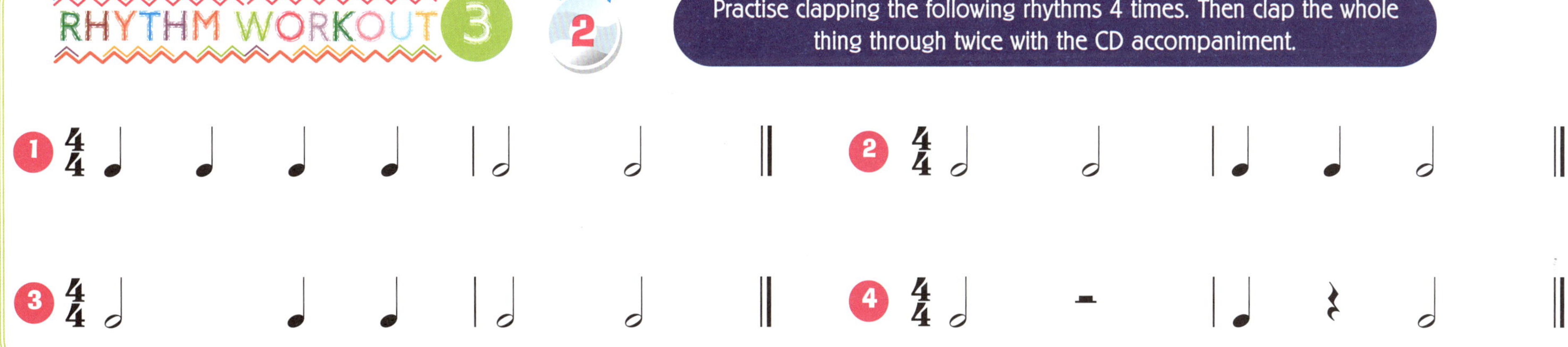

To make really good progress try to practise your flute every day.

Sunset beach

When you first start learning to play you may get tired. Just put your flute down for a while and have a short rest.

14

Music quiz

Let's see how much you have learnt about music so far.

Write your answers in the boxes below

1. How many beats is this note worth?

2. What is this sign called?

3. How many lines are there on a stave?

4. How many beats will there be in each bar?

5. What is a two-beat note called?
(clue: you can read this word backwards too!)

6. For how many beats should you rest when you see this sign?

7. What are these called?

8. For how many beats should you rest when you see this sign?

How many did you get right?
If you got some wrong see if you can find the
answers in Set 1 before going on to Set 2.

SET 2
Next note - A

This is what A looks like on the stave

○ This is a four beat note – a semibreve.

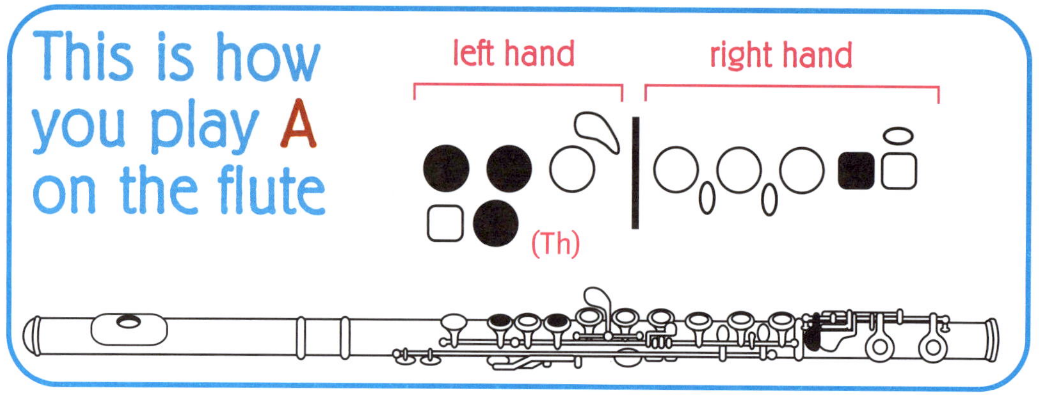

Lightly squeeze the necessary keys to get the note that you need. The fingers not being used should be gently touching their keys but not actually pressing them down. (see pages 8 and 9) for finger positions.

When you take off your middle finger (going to B after playing A) just move it the smallest amount possible and try to ensure that your fingertip keeps contact with the key. If you move your fingers as little as possible you'll be able to play fast pieces eventually.

Know the notes

Practise each of these patterns four times

1

2

3

4

Winter morning

TRACK 13 COMPLETE

TRACK 14 BACKING

Gently

Sunrise island

Using the notes B and A listen to the CD and try to copy the tunes like an echo.

When you learn about music you also have to learn to speak some Italian too!
Many of the words that tell you how the music should be played will be written in Italian.

piano is the Italian word for **soft**. It is written in the music as *p*.

forte is the Italian word for **loud**. It will say *f* on your music.

Just practise for short amounts of time when you first start learning to play the flute.

Cloudy skies

With sadness

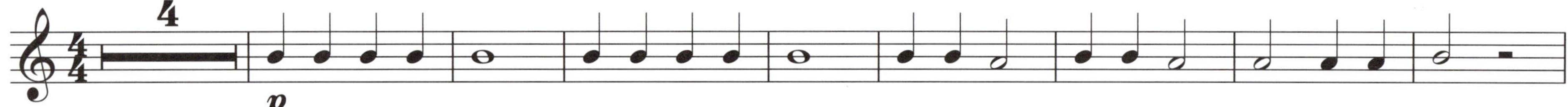

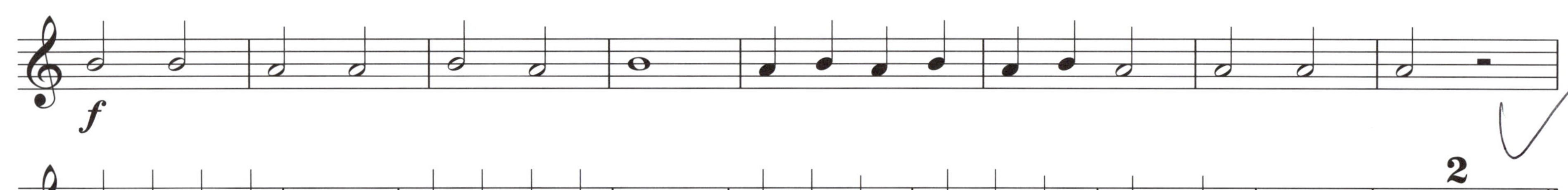

Wordsearch fun!

See if you can find the following musical words in the wordsearch.

CLEF   FLUTE   NOTES   PIANO
REST   MINIM   MUSIC   BAR
FORTE   STAVE   BEAT   TREBLE

M	I	N	I	M	U	B	E
B	E	A	T	U	O	A	T
N	O	T	E	S	S	F	R
O	E	R	P	I	A	N	O
A	T	E	R	C	L	E	F
W	U	B	A	R	E	D	A
R	L	L	P	T	S	E	R
S	F	E	V	A	T	S	N

This is a whole bar's rest. It hangs from the 4th line of the stave.

Get ready

Pupil

* Optional 2nd part

19

* Optional part for your teacher

SET 3
And now for – G

This is what G looks like on the stave

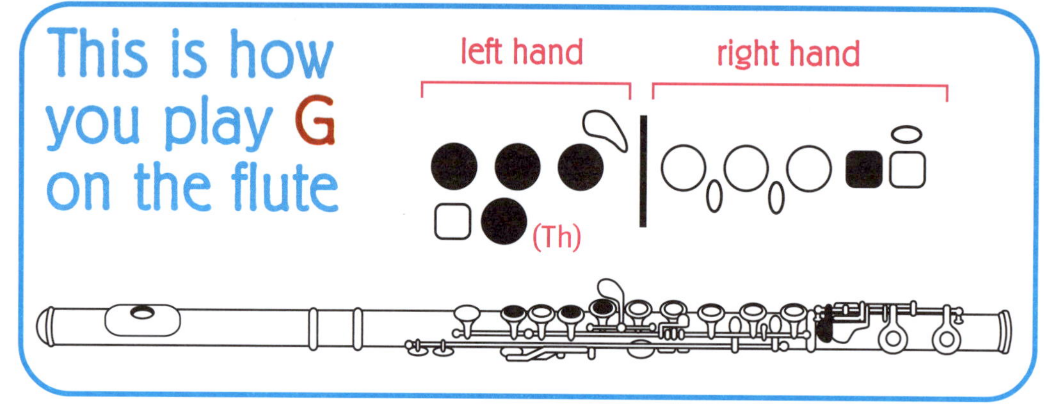

Know the notes Practise each of these patterns four times

1

2

3

This is a half-beat note – a quaver.

Two of them together are played in the time of one beat.

Cowboy's swing

4

f

p

f

Practise clapping the rhythms 4 times each. Then clap the whole thing through twice with the CD accompaniment.
If you want to go at a steady speed use CD track 2 but for a faster challenge use track 6 instead.

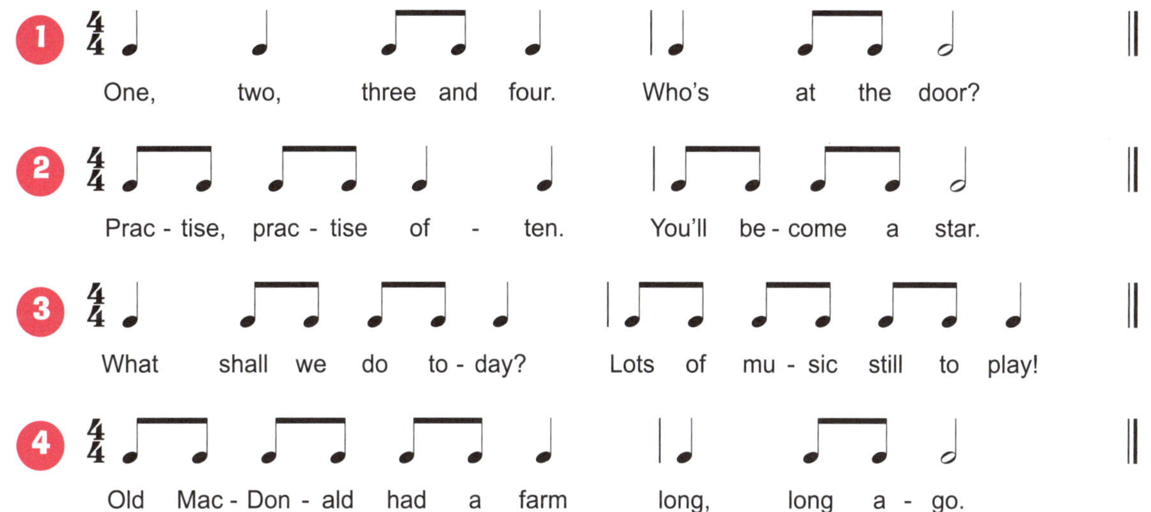

 **Listening game 2**

Using the notes B, A and G listen to the CD and try to copy the tunes like an echo.

Breathe in through your mouth – not your nose!

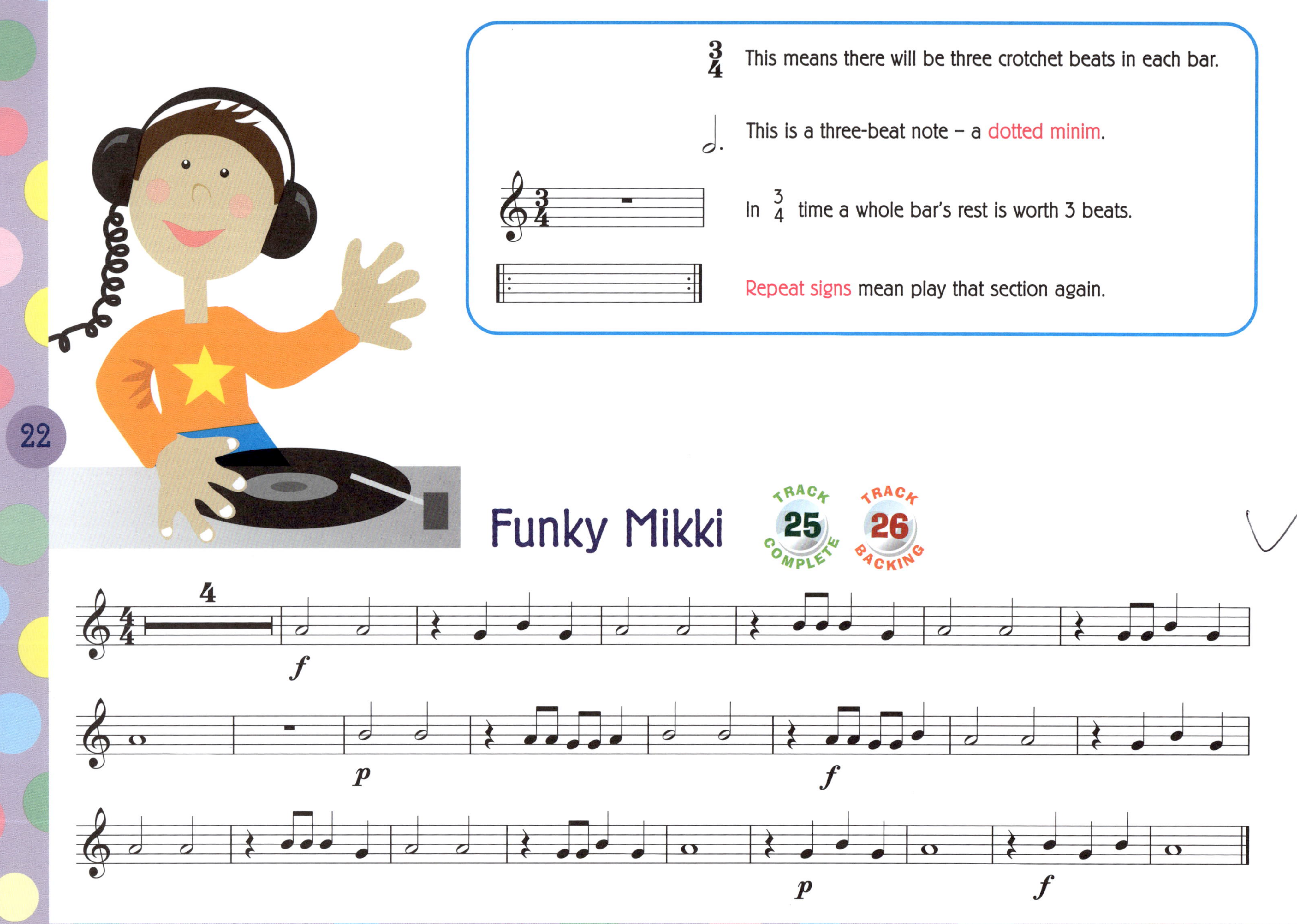

3/4 This means there will be three crotchet beats in each bar.

This is a three-beat note – a dotted minim.

In 3/4 time a whole bar's rest is worth 3 beats.

Repeat signs mean play that section again.

TRACK 25 COMPLETE
TRACK 26 BACKING
4
f
p
f
p
f

Funky Mikki

William's waltz

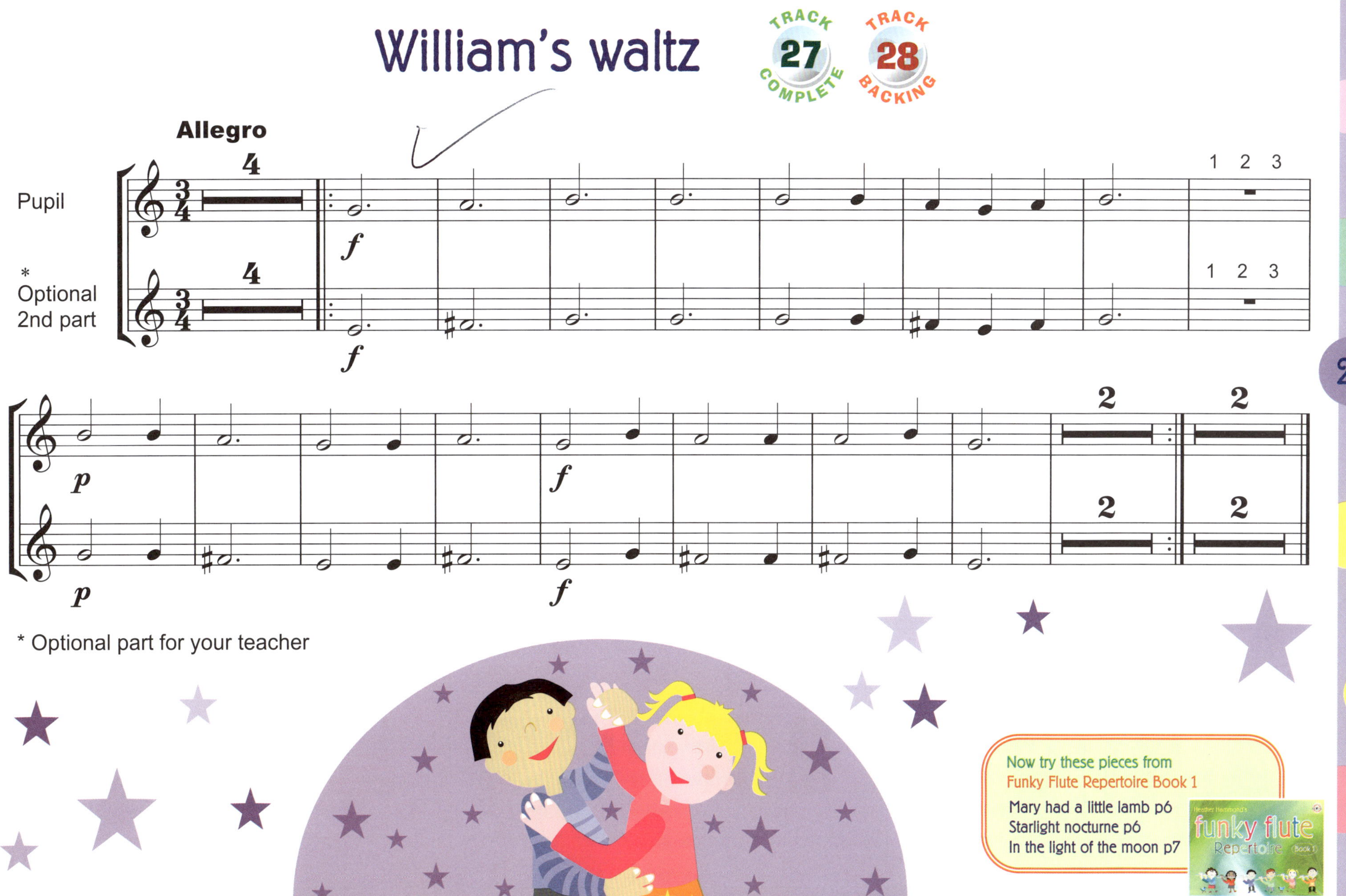

* Optional part for your teacher

Now try these pieces from
Funky Flute Repertoire Book 1

Mary had a little lamb p6
Starlight nocturne p6
In the light of the moon p7

Heading south
TRACK 29 COMPLETE
TRACK 30 BACKING
Allegro
f
1 2 3
1 2 3
p
24
Capital city problem!
Can you match the capitals with their countries using their correct rhythms?
Capital cities: Amsterdam / Paris / London / Rome / Copenhagen / Washington D.C.
Write your answers in the boxes below.
N
E
S
W
FRANCE
DENMARK
ITALY
UNITED KINGDOM
USA
NETHERLANDS

SET 4
Here's – C

This is what C looks like on the stave

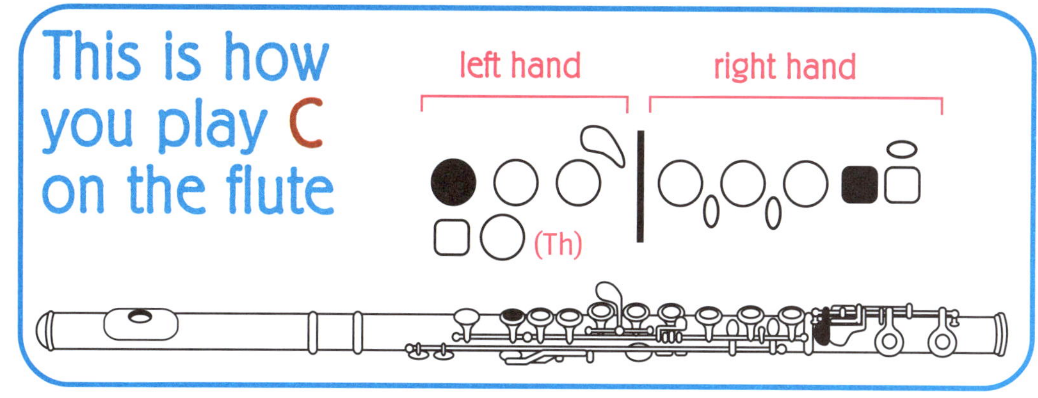

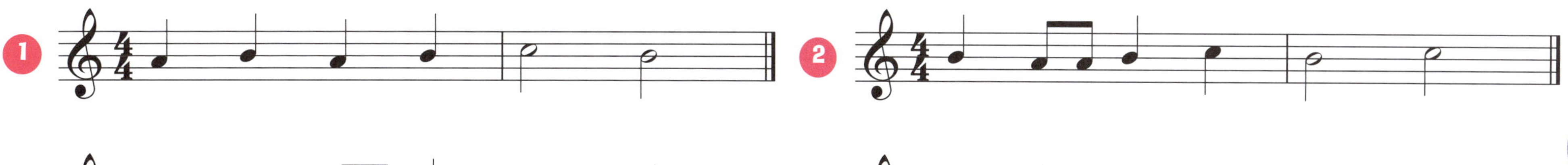

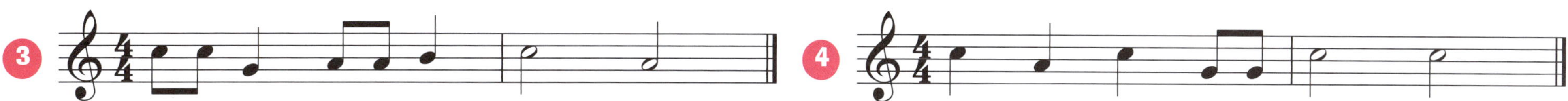

Using the notes C, B, A and G listen to the CD and try to copy the tunes.
They all start on C.

Don't forget to check whether you should be playing loudly f or softly p

Gradually get louder (also referred to as a **crescendo**).

Gradually get softer (also referred to as a **diminuendo**).

If there are only end repeat signs written you go right back to the beginning of the piece and play again.

Try these exercises to help you gradually change your loudness

Practise starting softly then gradually increase the air pressure and get louder throughout each bar. Take a breath each time you begin a new bar.

Practise starting loudly then gradually getting softer in each bar. You'll have to judge exactly how much air pressure to use to get a loud note that sounds good. Too much air may result in a much higher note than the one you should be playing!

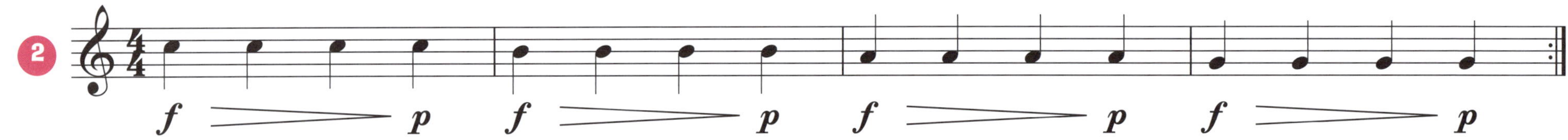

Next try making one long note gradually get louder. Remember to start each note by saying 't' gently and then gradually increase the air pressure throughout each four-beat note.

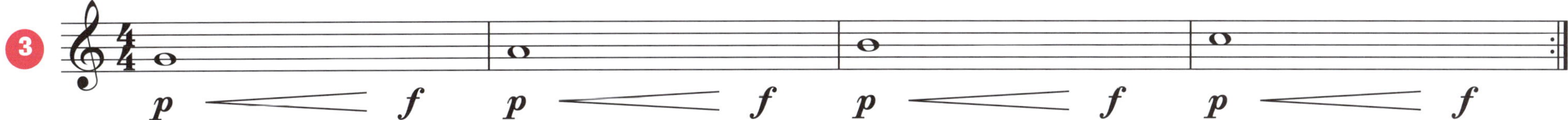

Start each note loudly then gradually get softer here.

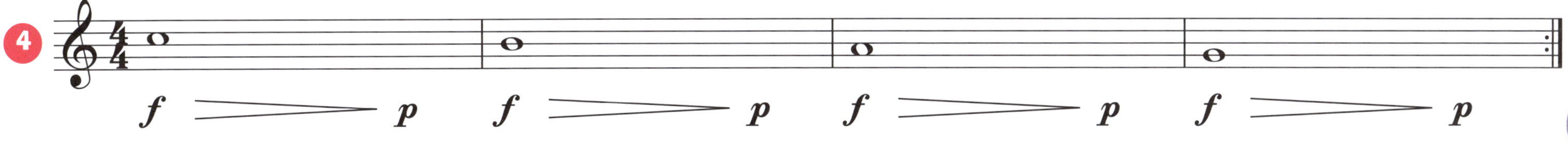

Finally play this short tune to practise gradually getting louder and softer as you play lots of different notes.

Always wipe off the moisture from your flute after you have finished playing.

Auntie's andante

Andante

Pupil

*Optional 2nd part

*Optional part for your teacher

19/05/20

Medieval march

Strange horizon

19/05/20

Play these long notes along with the CD. Try to make a really good sound. Breathe after each note if you need to.
Start playing after the 8-beat drum introduction.

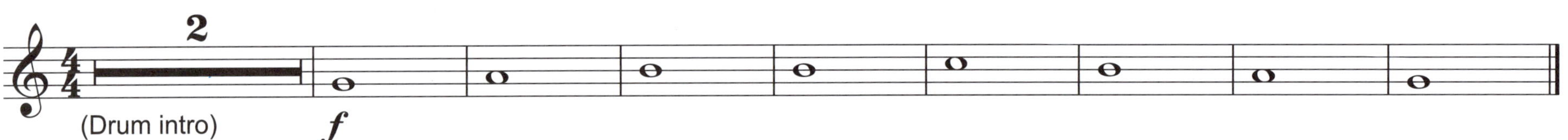

mezzo forte (*mf*) means play quite loudly – not as loudly as *f* though.

mezzo piano (*mp*) means play quite softly – not as softly as *p* though.

Monday morning waltz

Check that you are still tonguing. Remember to say 't' as you play each note.

Now try these pieces from
Funky Flute Repertoire Book 1

Brave and bold p8
Feelin' sad p9

First see how many answers you know without looking back in the book. If you do get stuck, all of the answers can be found earlier in this book.

1. The name of a two beat note.
2. This means 'quite soft' in Italian.
3. This appears at the beginning of the music and tells you how many beats there will be in every bar.
4. A piece of music with 3 beats in every bar is sometimes called this.
5. The time name of this note. 
6. The name of a note that is worth only half a beat.
7. This Italian word means 'medium walking speed'.
8. This Italian word tells you to play loudly.
9. What must you do for a whole bar when you see this sign?
10. How many beats is a minim worth?
11. Music is split into these with bar lines.
12. How many beats is this note worth?

SET 5
This is – F

This is what F looks like on the stave

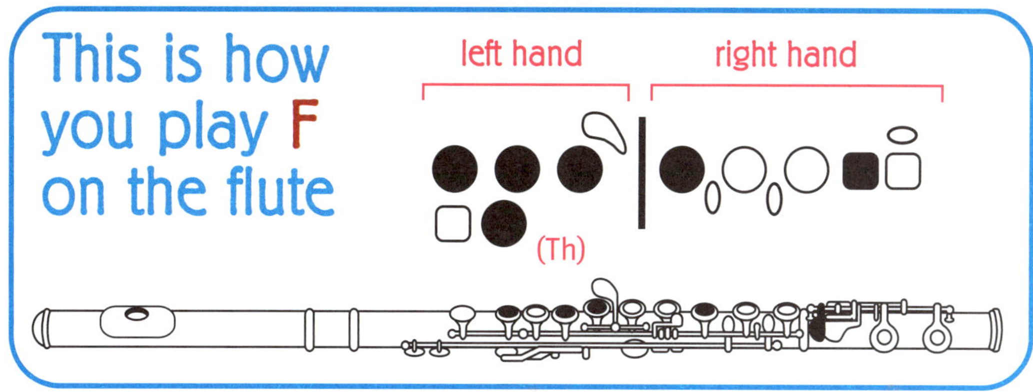

Know the notes

Practise each of these patterns four times

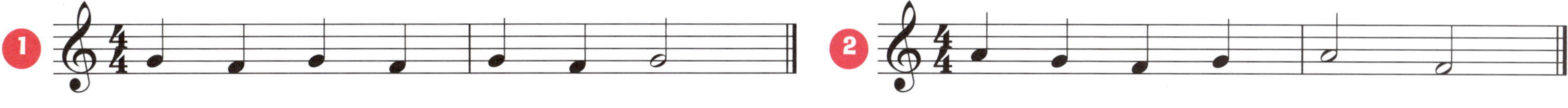

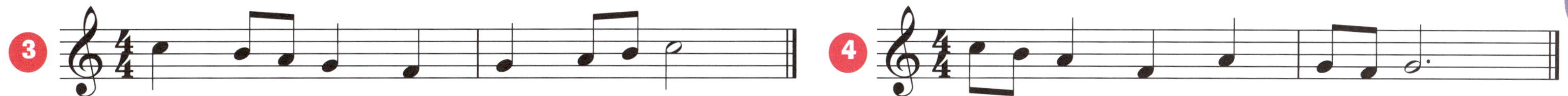

Practise clapping each of these rhythms four times. (Watch out for the rests!)
Then clap the whole thing through twice with the CD accompaniment. For a steady speed use track 2, for a faster speed try track 6.

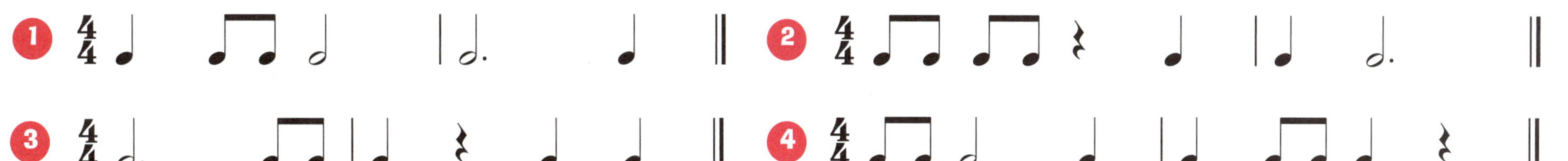

33

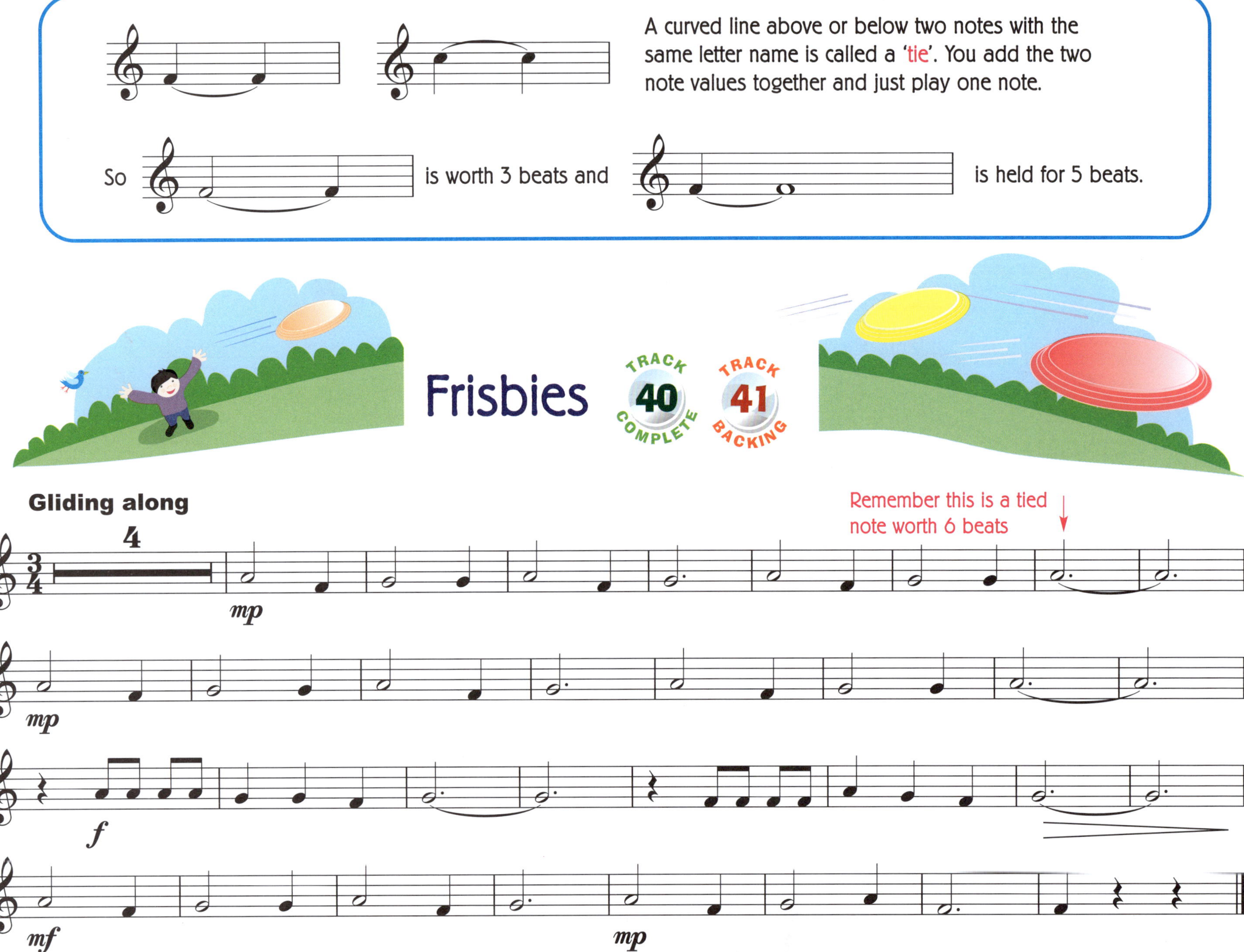

A curved line above or below two notes with the same letter name is called a 'tie'. You add the two note values together and just play one note.

So [notation] is worth 3 beats and [notation] is held for 5 beats.

Frisbies

Gliding along

mp

mp

f

mf

mp

Bluebirds

Dreamy andante

Rock pool bay

Rocky allegro

36

Quiz time

At Rock Pool Bay the ice-cream seller has forgotten which flavour each of the ice creams are. Can you use the rhythms to help him work out which is which?

Flavour	Ice-cream number
Tutti-frutti	7
Neapolitan	3
Choc-chip cookie	6
Bubblegum	9
Marshmallow	4
Blueberry pie	1
Toffee	8
Mint	2
Apple pie and custard	5

SET 6
And next is – B flat

This is what B flat (B♭) looks like on the stave 

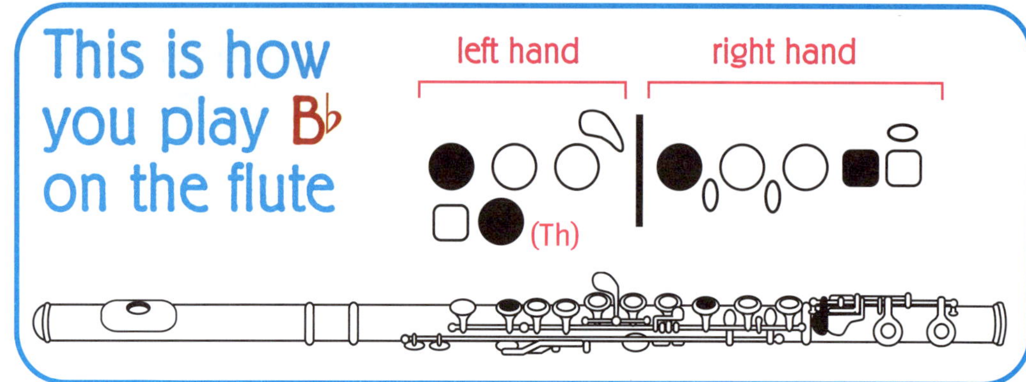

38

Know the notes
Practise each of these patterns four times
Don't forget the B flat!
1
2
3
4
60 seconds ballad
TRACK 47 COMPLETE
TRACK 48 BACKING
39
Pop ballad
4
mf
f
mp
mf
f
mp
Listening game 4
TRACK 49
Using the notes G and A, B♭ and C listen to the phrases on the CD and try to copy them. The first one starts on G.
Now try this piece from Funky Flute Repertoire Book 1
Girls and boys p11
funky flute Repertoire Book 1

Practise clapping each of these rhythms four times. Then clap the whole thing through with the CD accompaniment. Watch out for the rests!

Quavers can sometimes be grouped in 4's

Lazy weekend waltz

Flowing lazily along

Breathe when you need to – if necessary make a long note slightly shorter in order to grab a breath.

This is a natural sign. It cancels out the flat and means that you play a normal B note instead (B natural). This lasts for the whole bar unless another accidental sign is introduced to change the note again. Watch out for the natural sign towards the end of the next piece!

Clowns' picnic

Playfully

Pupil

* Optional 2nd part

* Optional part for your teacher

41

Happy or sad? Correct or wrong?

The clowns have been learning about music but they've got some of their information wrong. Can you help them to sort out their facts?

If the clown's information is correct draw a happy mouth and colour his hat yellow. If the clown's information is wrong draw a sad mouth and colour his hat red.

SET 7
Now for – E

This is what E looks like on the stave 

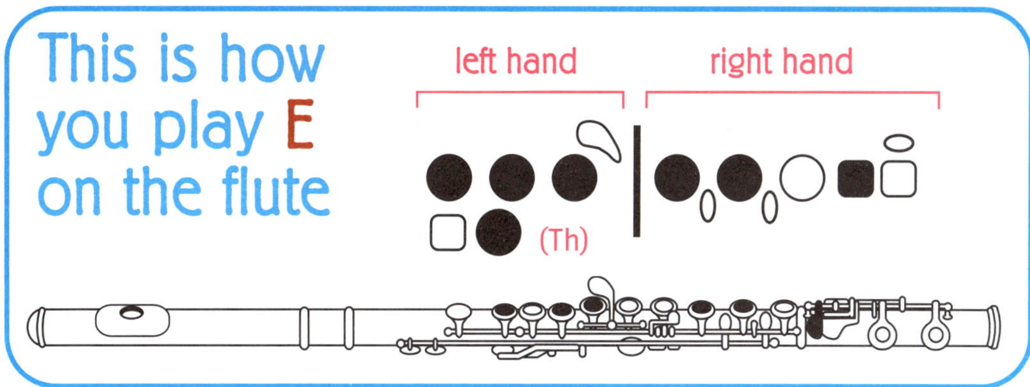

Know the notes

Practise each of these patterns four times

Diminuendo is the Italian word for gradually get softer. It is sometimes abbreviated to **dim**.

Crescendo means gradually get louder. It will sometimes just say **cresc.** in the music.

Moderato means play at a moderate speed.

D.S. al Coda means go back to the 𝄋 sign. You then play until you reach the **To Coda** ⊕ instruction. Then go to the coda (the end section).

It's quite difficult to play low notes loudly on the flute. If you blow with too much pressure you may get a much higher note than the one you're actually trying to play.

You might just need to play low notes softly first – but don't worry, as you become more experienced you'll eventually be able to play them louder.

The natural sign in bar 8 is a cautionary sign to remind you not to play a B flat after the previous bar.

Butternut bossa

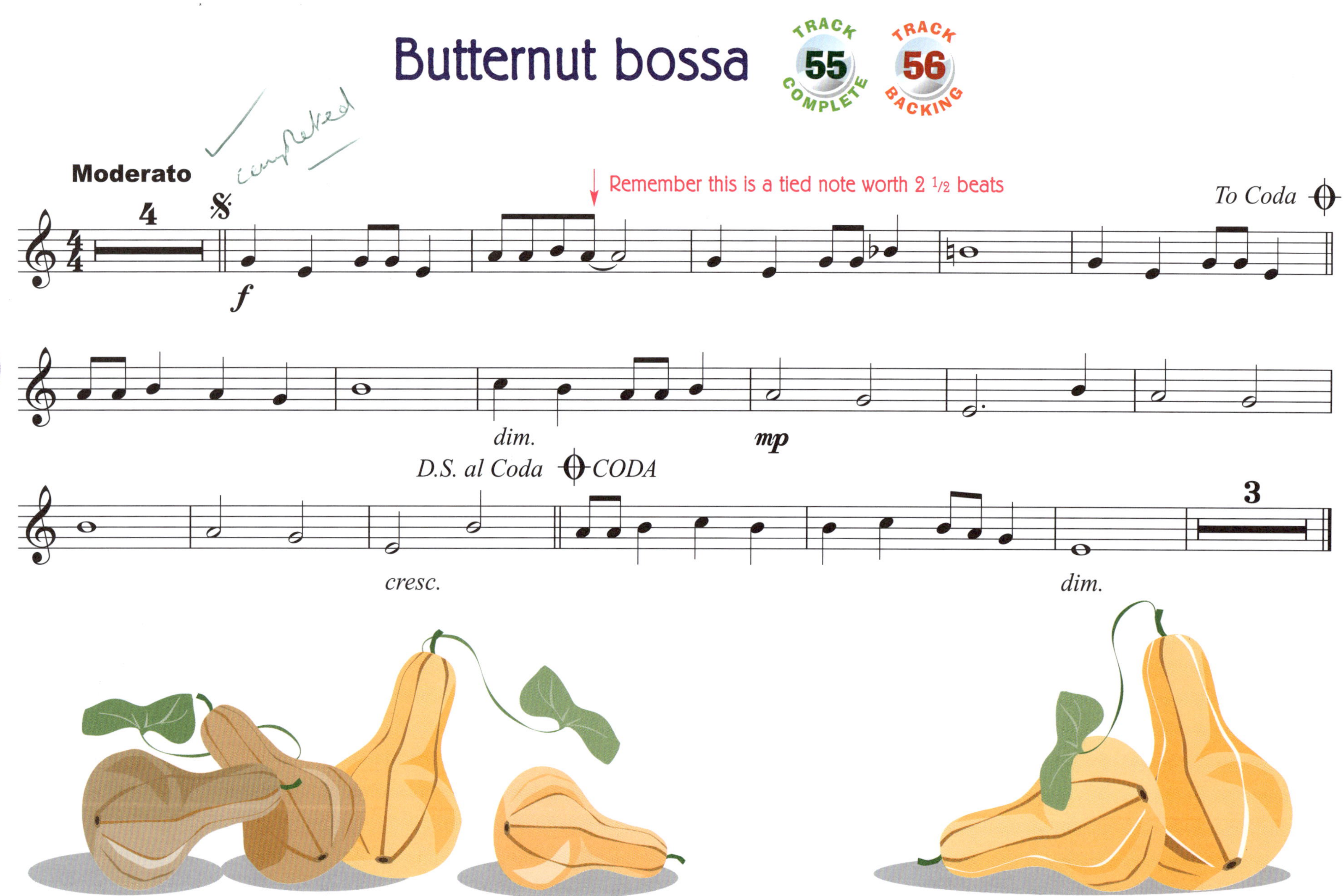

44

Play these long notes along with the CD. Try to get the best sound that you can.

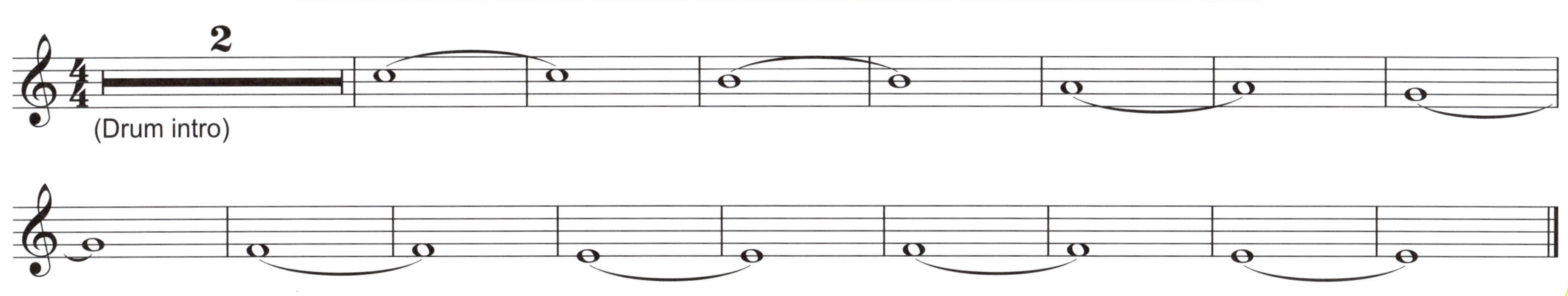

Keep a steady beat – Tapping your foot along with the music may help.

Practise clapping each of these rhythms four times. Then clap the whole thing through twice using your choice of accompaniment.

Wonderful

Relaxed moderato

> This is an accent. You play the note with extra force.

Aliens' clog dance

Allegro

mf

f

mp   f

47

Aliens landing
Help the aliens land their space ships in the correct places.
Draw a line between each alien space ship and its correct landing pad.
48
moderato
allegro
F
E
>
diminuendo
crescendo
lively
flat sign
moderate speed
play loudly
coda sign
accent
getting softer
natural sign

SET 8
Here is – F sharp

This is what F sharp (F#) looks like on the stave 

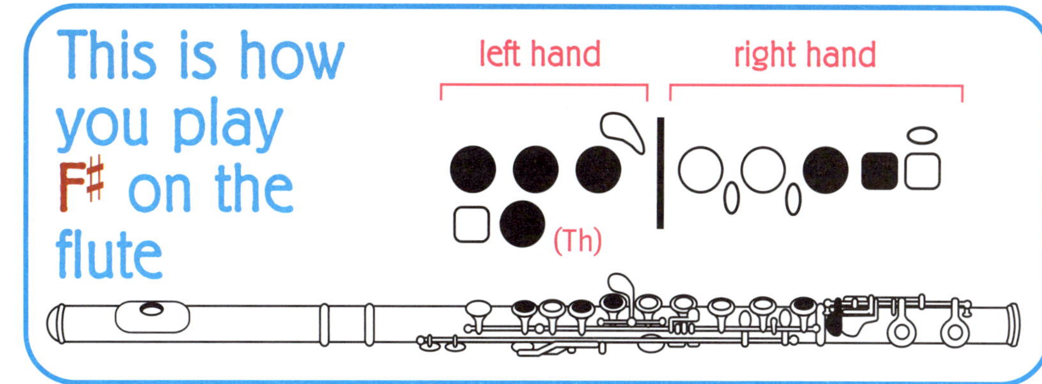

♯ This is a sharp sign – it makes the note slightly higher than it usually is.

Try this exercise so that you can hear how F sharp sounds compared with an ordinary F.

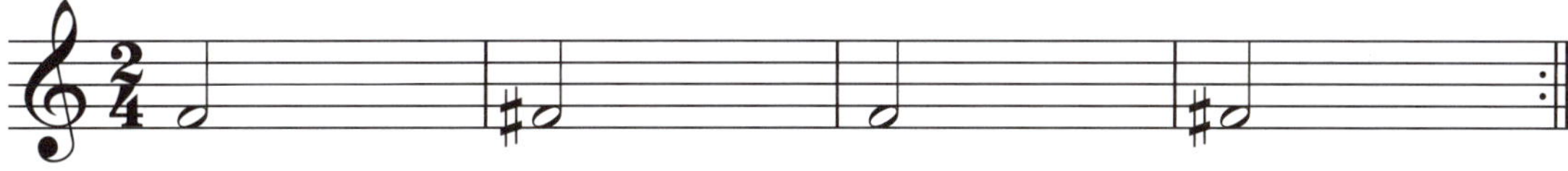

 This key signature is telling us that all of the F's in the pieces will be F sharps! (not ordinary F's).

Before you start to play always check the key signature to see if you should be playing any of the notes as flats or sharps.

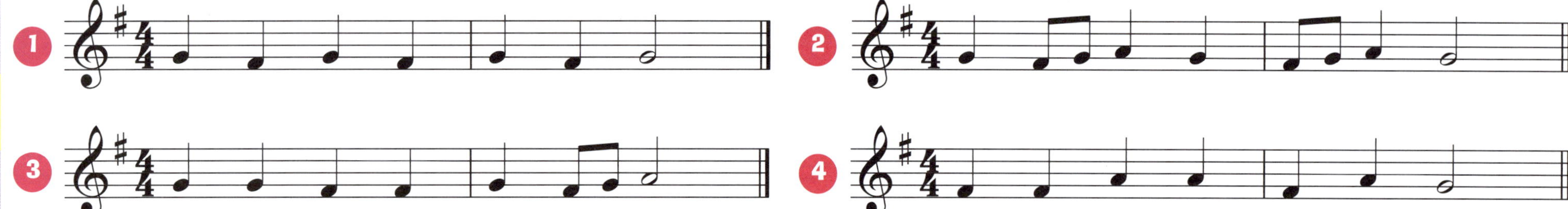

This is a slur. It tells you to play smoothly. You tongue the first note then move smoothly to the next note without tonguing it. It is sometimes called playing legato.

Slurs can also be placed above or below lots of notes. Just tongue the first one.

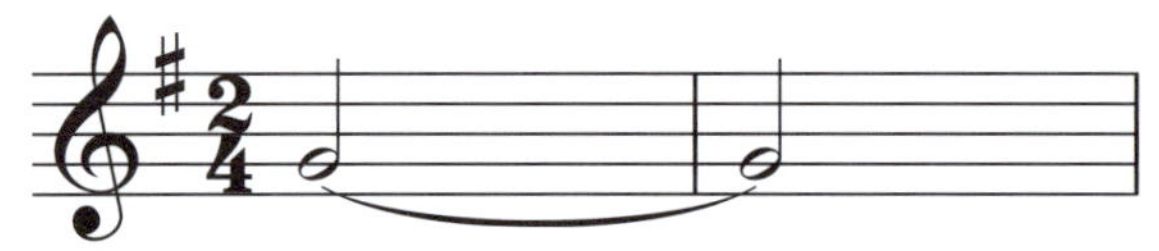

Don't forget that the same sign is used for tied notes too but both notes have to be the same letter name for it to be a tie.

Just can't wait

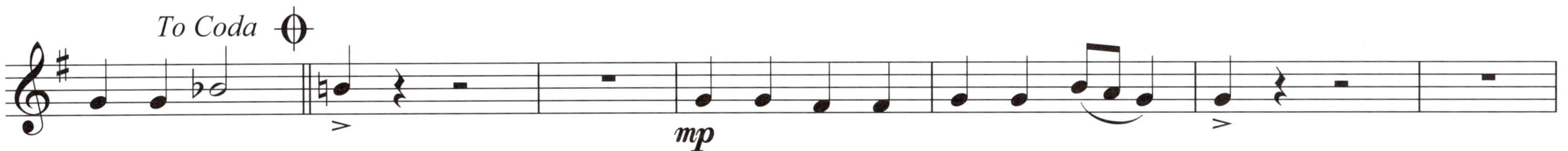

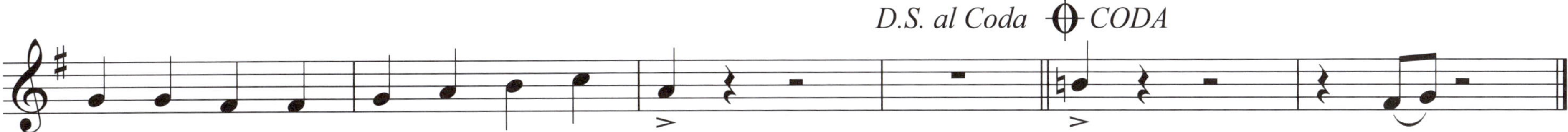

RHYTHM WORKOUT 8

Practise clapping each of these rhythms four times with a friend or your teacher. Count carefully.
Do a second time but change parts. Then clap the whole thing through using your choice of accompaniment.

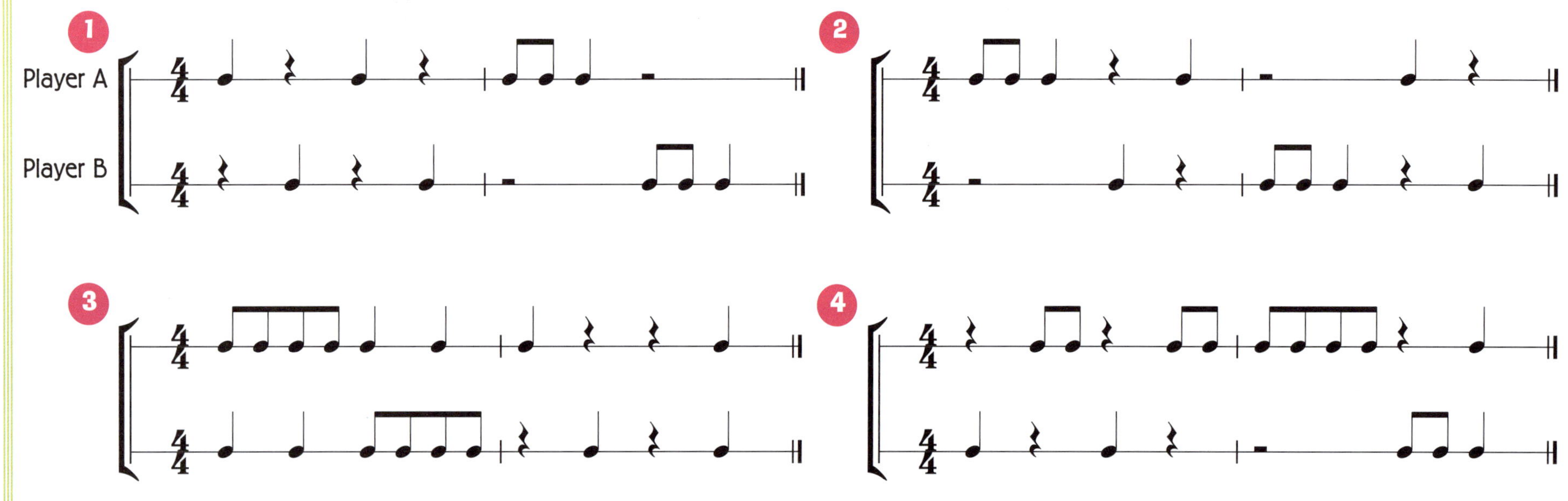

Using the notes B and A, G and F♯ listen to the phrases on the
CD and try to copy them. The first one starts on G.

Remember that getting the correct rhythm is just as important as playing the right notes!

Cop chase

Fast

Pupil

*Optional
2nd part

f

To Coda

f

mp

f

mp

D.S. al Coda CODA

cresc.

53

* Optional part for your teacher

A dot either below or above a note tells you to play it as a really short note. It's called staccato.

In the next tune there are lots of short notes for you to practise your staccato playing. Also watch out for the F sharps which appear from the end of the first line.

A change of key signature within a piece is indicated by a double bar line, followed by the new key signature.

Mrs Muddle

54

Fairly quick with a steady beat

Remember the F sharps!

Mrs Muddle's mix-up

Oh dear! Mrs Muddle seems to have got all of her musical words mixed up. Can you help her to unscramble them?

MRS MUDDLE'S WORD	CLUE	REAL WORD
RULS	the sign that tells you to play smoothly	
PARSH	the sign that makes the note slightly higher	
ADOC	the ending	
GELAROL	the Italian word for quick and lively playing	
TECCAN	tells you to play the note with extra force	
TALF	the sign that makes the note slightly lower	
TOMODEAR	this means play at a moderate speed	
ALUTARN	cancels out sharps and flats	
OCCERNEDS	gradually getting louder	
CATOCAST	this means play a short note	
TILNES	use your ears to do this whenever you play music	

SET 9
Time to learn – high D

This is what D looks like on the stave

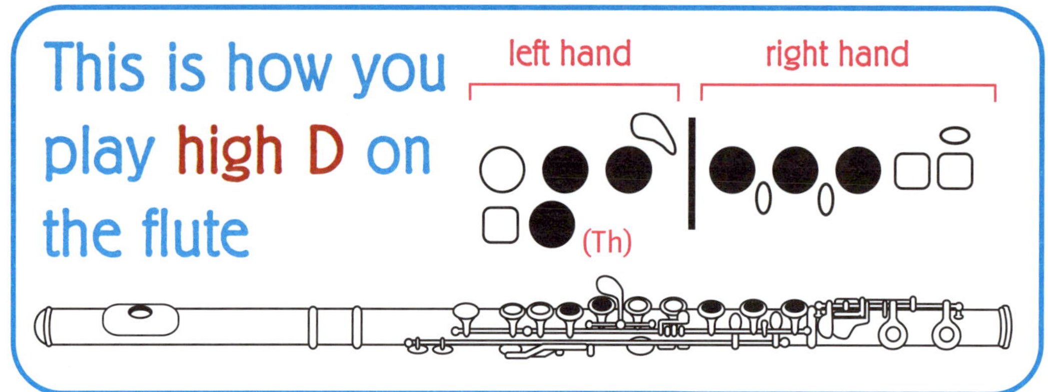

Know the notes

Practise each of these patterns four times. You may need to play them quite slowly first.

56

1

2

3

4

1st time and 2nd time bars – when you play the music the first time go to the 1st time bars, you then have to go back to the repeat sign.

When you are playing through for the 2nd time miss out the 1st time bars and go directly to the 2nd time bars.

This is a pause sign. It tells you to hold the note for a little while longer than it is actually worth.

DD boogie pants

With a driving Boogie beat

 Listening game 6

Using the notes G, A, B, C and D listen to the phrases on the CD and try to copy them. The first one starts on D.

Play along with the CD. Don't forget to concentrate on getting the best sound that you can.

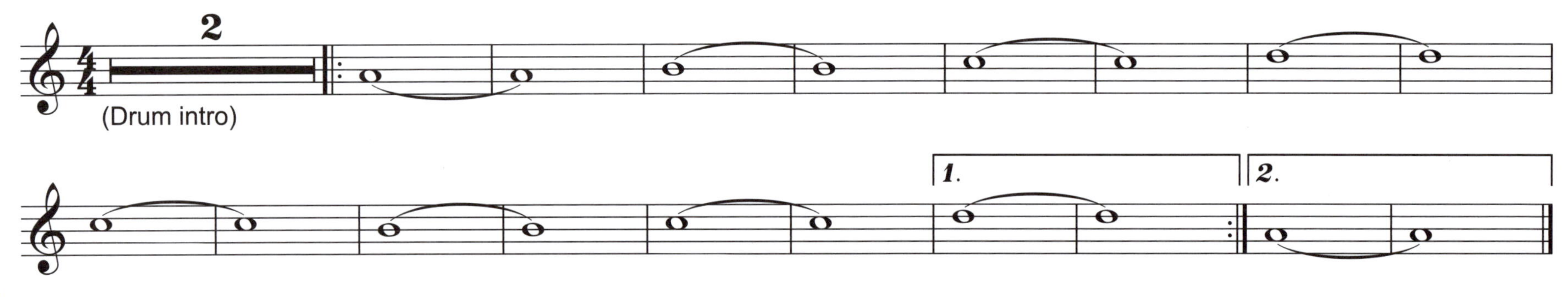

rall. means becoming gradually slower. It is short for the Italian word rallentando.

a tempo tells you to return to the original speed again.

If you find a new piece difficult when you first start practising it – just go very slowly for a while. As you get to know the piece more you'll gradually find that you can play it at the correct speed.

Now try these pieces from
Funky Flute Repertoire Book 1

Misty mood p23
This old man p24
While shepherds watched their flocks p24
Kit bag blues p25

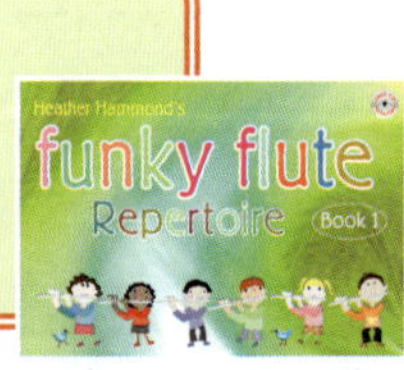

Ballad for Mr Blue
TRACK 73 COMPLETE
TRACK 74 BACKING
Gently flowing
a tempo
mp
mf
To Coda
f
rall.
D.S. al Coda
CODA
rall.
p
59

Sounds familiar?

Can you add the missing items to complete this well-known tune?

1. Put a B flat in the key signature.
2. Put in a time signature that means 4 crotchet beats in every bar.
3. Add an F crotchet.
4. Add a bar line.
5. Add a B flat note worth 3 beats here.
6. Add an F worth 2 beats.
7. Add a rest worth 1 beat.
8. Add a B flat note worth 1 beat.
9. Add 4 crotchet B flats in this bar.
10. Add a B flat crotchet here.
11. Add an F minim here.
12. Add a C crotchet.
13. Add a B flat note worth 4 beats.
14. Now play the tune.
15. Add the title above the tune.

60

Song title:

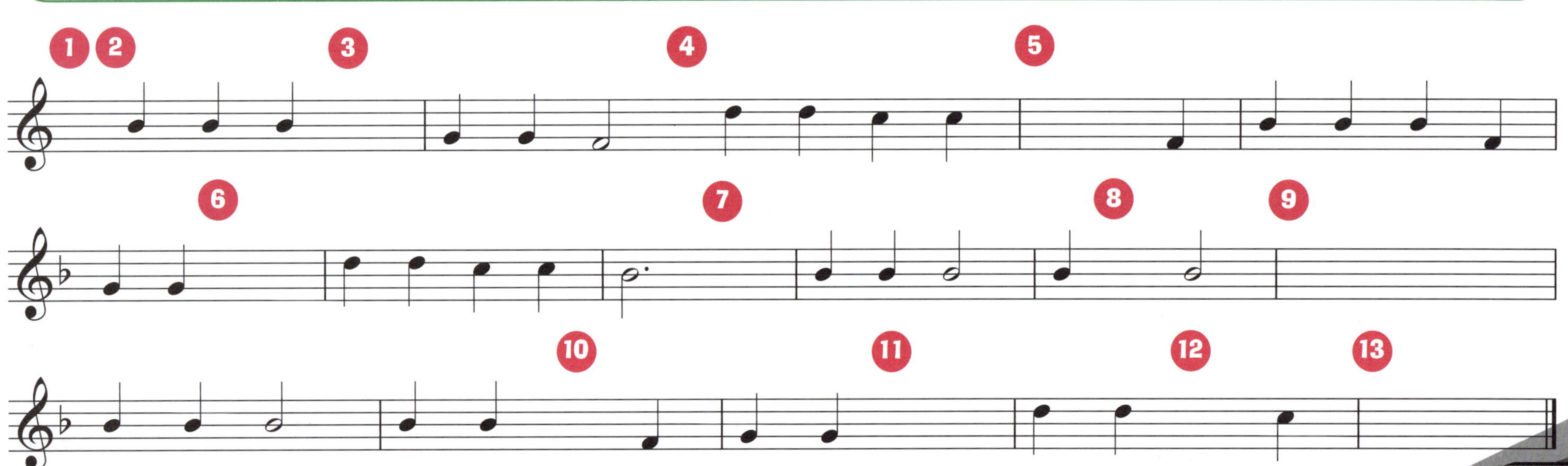

Engineer's rag

Moving along

61

Never dance with an elephant!

Not too fast

This tune uses all of the 9 notes that you know!

mp

mf

To Coda

f

p

D.S. al Coda

mp

mf

f

CODA

f

p

mf

f

62

Now try these pieces from
Funky Flute Repertoire Book 1

Lucky boots bossa p26
Lavender's blue p29
Frère Jacques trio p30

This is to certify that

____

has successfully completed

Funky Flute Book 1

and is now promoted to **Funky Flute Book 2**

____
Teacher

____
Date